Lovers of the Lost

Lovers of the Lost

NEW & SELECTED POEMS BY

Wesley McNair

DAVID R. GODINE · *Publisher* · *Boston*

First published in 2010 by
David R. Godine · *Publisher*
Post Office Box 450
Jaffrey, New Hampshire 03452
www.godine.com

LIBRARY OF CONGRESS
CATALOGING-IN-PUBLICATION DATA
McNair, Wesley.
Lovers of the lost : new & selected poems / by Wesley McNair. -- 1st ed.
p.   cm.
ISBN 978-1-56792-398-8
I. Title.
PS3563.C388L68 2010
813'.54—dc22
2009022387

FIRST EDITION
Printed in the United States of America

Contents

from THE FACES OF AMERICANS IN 1853

   Small Towns Are Passing · 13
   Mina Bell's Cows · 14
   The Bald Spot · 14
   Hair on Television · 16
   The Thugs of Old Comics · 17
   The Faces of Americans in 1853 · 18
   Where I Live · 20

from THE TOWN OF NO

   The Last Time Shorty Towers
      Fetched the Cows · 23
   Mute · 24
   Killing the Animals · 25
   Ghosts · 25
   The Man with the Radios · 28
   The Faith Healer · 30
   The Before People · 32
   A Traveler's Advisory · 33
   What It Is · 34
   Hearing That My Father
      Died in a Supermarket · 35
   After My Stepfather's Death · 37
   The Abandonment · 38
   When Paul Flew Away · 38
   Happiness · 41

from MY BROTHER RUNNING

Young Man Going Uphill with a Bird · 45
The Secret · 46
The Life · 48
Seeing Mercer, Maine · 48
Making Things Clean · 50
The One Who Will Save You · 51
Reading Poems at the Grange Meeting
    in What Must Be Heaven · 53

from TALKING IN THE DARK

This Love Song · 59
Old Guys · 59
Old Cadillacs · 61
The Puppy · 62
Trying to Find Her Teeth · 62
The Book of A · 63
Weeds · 65
Waving Goodbye · 66
Glass Night · 67
The Characters of Dirty Jokes · 68
Poem for My Feet · 70
The Retarded Children Play Baseball · 71
Why We Need Poetry · 72
Love Handles · 73

from FIRE

    How I Became a Poet · 79
    The Good-Boy Suit · 79
    Shovels · 81
    The One I Think of Now · 83
    Sleep · 84
    Voiceless · 84
    Speech · 86
    An Executive's Afterlife · 87
    Smoking · 88
    History of Talking on the Phone · 90
    What Became · 92
    The Rules of the New Car · 93
    Goodbye to the Old Life · 94
    Charles by Accident · 96
    Driving North in Winter · 98

from THE GHOSTS OF YOU AND ME

    My Father Going Away · 103
    The Boy Carrying the Flag · 105
    Kuhre's Farm · 108
    It · 112
    Hymn to the Comb-Over · 113
    The Gangsters of Old Movies · 114
    The 1950s · 116
    The Last Black and White TV · 118
    If You Had Come · 120

As Long As We Remember Him
    He Will Never Die · 121
Mistakes about Heaven · 124
My Mother Enters Heaven · 126
The Man He Turned Into · 128
That Nothing · 130
As I Am · 131
My Town · 132
Love Poem · 134

THE LOVER: NEW POEMS

For My Wife · 139
November 22, 1963 · 140
What She Means · 141
Losing My Hair · 142
Shame · 143
Morning in America · 145
The Lover · 147
Her Secret · 148
First Snowfall · 152
Love Story · 154

Acknowledgments · 156

for Diane

FROM *The Faces of Americans in 1853*

Small Towns Are Passing

Small towns are passing
into the rearview
mirrors of our cars.
The white houses
are moving away,
wrapping trees
around themselves,
and stores are taking
their gas pumps
down the street
backwards. Just like that
whole families picnicking
on their lawns tilt
over the hill,
and kids on bikes
ride toward us
off the horizon,
leaving no trace
of where they have gone.
Signs turn back and start
after them. Packs of mailboxes,
like dogs, chase them
around corner after corner.

Mina Bell's Cows

O where are Mina Bell's cows who gave no milk
and grazed on her dead husband's farm?
Each day she walked with them into the field,
loving their swayback dreaminess more
than the quickness of any dog or chicken.
Each night she brought them grain in the dim barn,
holding their breath in her hands.
O when the lightning struck Daisy and Bets,
her son dug such great holes in the yard
she could not bear to watch him.
And when the baby, April, growing old
and wayward, fell down the hay chute,
Mina just sat in the kitchen, crying "Ape,
Ape," as if she called all three cows,
her walleyed girls who never would come home.

The Bald Spot

It nods
behind me
as I speak
at the meeting.

All night
while I sleep
it stares
into the dark.

The bald spot
is bored.
Tired of waiting
in the office,

sick of following me
into sex.
It traces
and retraces

itself,
dreaming
the shape
of worlds

beyond its world.
Far away
it hears the laughter
of my colleagues,

the swift sure
sound of my voice.
The bald spot
says nothing.

It peers
out from hair
like the face
of a doomed man

going blanker
and blanker,
walking backwards
into my life.

Hair on Television

On the soap opera the doctor
explains to the young woman with cancer
that each day is beautiful.

Hair lifts from their heads
like clouds, like something to eat.

It is the hair of the married couple getting in touch
with their real feelings for the first time
on the talk show,

the hair of young people on the beach
drinking Cokes and falling in love.

And the man who took the laxative and waters his garden
next day with the hose wears the hair

so dark and wavy even his grandchildren are amazed,
and the woman who never dreamed tampons
could be so convenient wears it.

For the hair is changing people's lives.
It is growing like wheat above the faces

of game show contestants opening the doors
of new convertibles, of prominent businessmen opening
their hearts to Christ, and it is growing

straight back from the foreheads of vitamin experts,
detergent and dog food experts
helping ordinary housewives discover

how to be healthier, get clothes cleaner,
and serve dogs meals they love in the hair.

And over and over on television the housewives,
and the news teams bringing all the news faster
and faster, and the new breed of cops winning the fight

against crime are smiling, pleased to be at their best,
proud to be among the literally millions of Americans

everywhere who have tried the hair, compared the hair,
and will never go back to life before the active,
the caring, the successful, the incredible hair.

The Thugs of Old Comics

At first the job is a cinch, like they said.
They manage to get the bank teller a couple of times
in the head and blow the vault door so high
it never comes down. Money bags line the shelves
inside like groceries. They are rich, richer
than they can believe. Above his purple suit the boss
is grinning half outside of his face.

Two goons are taking the dough in their arms
like their first women. For a minute nobody sees
the little thug with the beanie is sweating drops
the size of hot dogs and pointing
straight up. There is a blue man flying
down through the skylight and landing with his arms
crossed. They exhale their astonishment
into small balloons. "What the," they say,
"What the," watching their bullets drop
off his chest over and over. Soon he begins to talk
about the fight against evil, beating them half to death
with his fists. Soon they are picking themselves up
from the floor of the prison. Out the window
Superman is just clearing a tall building
and couldn't care less when they shout
his name through the bars. "We're trapped!
We got no chance!" they say, tightening their teeth,

thinking, like you, how it always gets down
to the same old shit: no fun, no dough,
no power to rise out of their bodies.

The Faces of Americans in 1853

Let us analyze the American. . . . The American head is gen-erally large, which the phrenologists attribute to increased development of the brain. There are all varieties of face, though the oval predominates. . . . The facial features are,

for the most part, more sharply chiseled with us than with
any other people.

"Are We a Good-Looking People?"

(1853)

When you turned
to the farmhand who hailed you
from the field, you could see the face
of the American.

Everyone had the face.
There was an appreciation
for the way each chin perfected
an oval.

All day in his shop
the blacksmith
swung his hammer laughing
at the nondescript faces of Europe.

At night in her home
the mother
admired the heads
of her children, already large.

As far away
as Kansas
their chiseled features rose
up from the horizon.

Indians who looked down at the faces
of those they had killed
with their arrows
wept at their mistake.

Where I Live

You will come into an antique town
whose houses move apart
as if you'd interrupted
a private discussion. This is the place
you must pass through to get there.
Imagining lives tucked in
like china plates, continue driving.
Beyond the landscaped streets,
beyond the last colonial gas station
and unsolved by zoning,
is a road. It will take you
to old farmhouses and trees
with car-tire swings.
Signs will announce hairdressing
and nightcrawlers.
The timothy grass will run beside you
all the way to where I live.

The Last Time Shorty Towers Fetched the Cows

In the only story we have
of Shorty Towers, it is five o'clock,
and he is dead drunk on his roof
deciding to fetch the cows. How
he got in this condition, shingling
all afternoon, is what the son-in-law,
the one who made the back pasture
into a golf course, can't figure out. So,
with an expression somewhere between shock
and recognition, he just watches Shorty
pull himself up to his not-so-
full height, square his shoulders,
and sigh that small sigh as if caught
once again in an invisible swarm
of bees. Let us imagine, in that moment
just before he turns to the roof's edge
and the abrupt end of the joke
which is all anyone thought to remember
of his life, Shorty is listening
to what seems to be the voice
of a lost heifer, just breaking
upward. And let us think that when he walks
with such odd purpose down that hill
jagged with shingles, he suddenly feels it
open into the wide, incredibly green
meadow where all the cows are.

Mute

Once, on the last ice-hauling,
the sled went through the surface
of the frozen pond,
pulling the son under
the thrashing hooves
of horses. Listening for him

after all her tears was perhaps
what drew the mother
into that silence. Long afternoons
she sat with the daughter,
speaking in the sign language
they invented together,
going deaf to the world.

How, exactly, did they touch
their mouths? What was the thought
of the old man on the porch
growing so drunk by nightfall
he could not hear
mosquitoes in his ears?

There is so much no one remembers
about the farm where sound,
even the bawling of the unmilked cows,
came to a stop. Even the man's name,

which neighbors must have spoken
passing by in twilight, on their way
to forgetting it forever.

Killing the Animals

The chickens cannot
find their heads
though they search for them,
falling in the grass.

And the great bulls
remain on their knees,
unable to remember
how to stand.

The goats cannot find their voices.
They run quickly
on their sides,
watching the sky.

Ghosts

When we went there,
the TV with the ghosts
would be on, and the father
talked and called out
every now and then to him,
sitting in that space
we always left around him,
Isn't it, June? Or *Aren't
you, June?* And June
would laugh like only his voice
was doing it and he was somewhere
else, so when the father

25

turned back to us like
he was enjoying his son's
company, we could tell
he was on his way out,
too. Until at the end
he just sat saying nothing
all day into the dark.
Walking by there after chores,
we would see the blue light
from their TV, shifting
across the road in the trees,
and inside, those two dark
heads which had forgot
by this time even the cows.
So when the truck came
to take the manure-matted,
bellowing things to the slaughterhouse,
all we could say was, Thank God
for Liz. Who else
would have helped load them up,
then gone right on living
with that brother and father, dead
to the world in bib overalls,
while all around them
the fields had begun
to forget they were fields?
Who else would have taken
that town job, punching
shoelace holes all night
into shoes? So now
when we went, there
would be Junior and his father

in the front room of the farm
they did not remember,
wearing brand-new shoes
they did not even know
they wore, watching the TV
with the ghosts. And there
would be Liz, with her apron on
over her pants, calling out
to them like they were only
deaf, *Isn't it?*
or *Aren't you?* and telling us
how at last they could have
no worries and be free.
And the thing was
that sometimes when we watched
them, watching those faces
which could no longer concentrate
on being faces, in the light
that shifted from news to ads
to sports, we could almost see
what she meant. But what
we didn't see was
that she also meant
herself. That the very
newspapers we sat on
each time we brought her milk
or eggs were Liz's own
slow way of forgetting all
the couches and chairs. Until
that last awful day
we went there,
after her father died,

and after the state car
came to take June,
and we found just flour-
bags and newspapers and Liz,
with her gray pigtail
coming undone, and no idea why
we'd left our rock-strewn fields
to come. Then all
we could think to do
was unplug that damned
TV, which by now didn't
have ghosts, only voices talking
beyond the continuous snow.
All we could do was
call her to come back
into her face and hands,
and Liz just watched
us, waving our arms,
like we weren't even there,
like we were the ghosts.

The Man with the Radios

Beyond the curtainless
bay windows of his room
on the side street,

he kneels
among old radios, left
from a time of belief

in radios,
some dangling fat
tails of cord

from end tables, some
in darkening corners
sprouting hairs of wire

from their great backs,
and this strange one
he has chosen,

standing on the paws
of an African cat.
The man with the radios

is so far away
in his gaze you would swear
he sees nothing,

so still you might miss
how he concentrates
on not moving

his hand. Slowly,
slowly he turns
its ridged

knob in the dark,
listening for the sound
he has prepared it for,

watching with his absent eyes
the film that clears
from a green eye.

The Faith Healer

When I turned,
it was like the father
had been walking right
toward me forever
with his eyes shut
pushing that boy,
all washed up and
dressed up and riding
above those long spokes
shooting light like
he was something more than arms
and a chest. Already
the mother was saying *please,*
oh please, partly to me,
partly because she heard
the sound, so soft
and far off at first
you might have never guessed it
was going to be the father
with his eyes shut, screaming.
But I knew, and I knew
even before it stopped
and he began to point
down at his son's

steel feet and whatever
was inside the dead
balloons of his pants,
the father did it. So when
he said he did it,
I was thinking of how
only his mouth was moving
in his shut face like
he had gone somewhere
outside of his body
which he could not stand.
And when he said
he did it because his son
burned the new barn down
to the ground, then shook
and shook so you could see
he was inside his body
and could never leave,
all I could think
was how the wind was moving
the tent. Lifting it up
and up around the father
who could not see it lifting,
and the mother with the no-
color dress, and that small,
still boy, all washed up
and dressed up and
looking right at me
almost like it was OK
being a chest. Which was the moment
when my own legs went out

from under me, and I woke
with the cold steel bars
of his wheelchair fast
in my hands, and shouting
like for the first
time, *heal, oh heal,*
over and over to the legs
that could not walk,
and to the legs
that could, and to everyone,
everywhere, who could never
get free from such sadness.

The Before People

There is a moment when they turn
to the ads that are meant for them
and are happy, a moment when the fat woman
thinks of melting her body away in seven days,
and the shut-in imagines big money
without leaving his home. Slowly,
as if for the first time, they read
the italics of their deepest wishes:
Made $5,000 in first month,
Used to call me Fatty, and all
the people with no confidence,
no breasts, or hair in the wrong places,
find pictures of the amazing results
in their own states. They have overlooked
the new techniques and the research

of doctors in Germany, they know that now,
suddenly so pleased they can hardly
remember being sad in this, their moment,
before, just before they lie back on the beds
in their small rooms and think about how foolish
they are or how farfetched it is or anything
except the actual photographs of their dreams.

A Traveler's Advisory

The main streets of towns
don't go uphill,
and the houses aren't
purple like that
tenement with one eye
clapboarded over. Never mind
how it wavers
backward, watching you
try to find second gear.
You've arrived
at the top of the town:
a closed gas station
where nobody's dog
sits, collarless,
and right next door
a church that seems
to advertise Unleaded.
Who's hung this
great front door
above no steps? No one

you'd know.
And what suspends
the avalanche
of barn? Nothing,
and you will never
escape the bump,
lifting shiny with tar.
And you won't
need the sign that says
you are leaving Don't Blink,
Can't Dance,
or Town of No.

What It Is

It is not what,
carrying that
afterthought of legs,
he runs to, and not
what his interrogative, foldy
face detects
on the floor, because
it is always changing, always
turning out to be
some other bug
or bush his nose wanted,
leaving his tail
smoldering
behind, and
it is never,

after all that scratching
and lifting of leg,
enough: not even
after he joins
the dinner party, smiling
upside-down
and rolling
his testicles, not even
in his whimpering sleep,
dreaming in the tips
of his paws
that he is chasing
it, that very thing
which, scratching,
he can't quite
reach, nor sniffing find,
because in the perfect
brainlessness of dog,
he will never know
what it is.

Hearing That My Father Died in a Supermarket

At first it is difficult
to see you
are dropping dead –

you seem lost
in thought, adjusting your tie
as if to rehearse

some imaginary speech
though of course beginning
to fall,

your mouth opening wider
than I have ever seen
a mouth,

your hands deep
in your shirt,
going down

into the cheeses, making the sound
that is not
my name,

that explains nothing
over and over,
going away

into your hands
into your face,
leaving this great body

on its knees,
the father
of my body

which holds me
in this world,
watching you go

on falling
through the Muzak,
making the sound

that is not my name,
that will never
explain anything, oh father,

stranger, all dressed up
and deserting me
for the last time.

After My Stepfather's Death

Again it is the moment before I left home
for good, and my mother is sitting quietly
in the front seat while my stepfather pulls me
and my suitcase out of the car and begins
hurling my clothes, though now
I notice for the first time how the wind
unfolds my white shirt and puts its slow
arm in the sleeve of my blue shirt and lifts them
all into the air above our heads so beautifully
I want to shout at him to stop and look up
at what he has made, but of course when I turn
to him, a small man, bitter even this young
that the world will not go his way, my stepfather
still moves in his terrible anger, closing the trunk,
and closing himself into the car as hard as he can,
and speeding away into the last years of his life.

The Abandonment

Climbing on top of him and breathing
into his mouth this way she could be showing her
desire except that when she draws back
from him to make her little cries
she is turning to her young son just
coming into the room to find his father my brother
on the bed with his eyes closed and the slightest
smile on his lips as if when they
both beat on his chest as they do now
he will come back from the dream he is enjoying
so much he cannot hear her calling his name
louder and louder and the son saying get up
get up discovering both of them discovering
for the first time that all along
he has lived in this body this thing
with shut lids dangling its arms
that have nothing to do with him and everything
they can ever know the wife listening weeping
at his chest and the mute son who will never
forget how she takes the face into her hands now
as if there were nothing in the world
but the face and breathes oh
breathes into the mouth which does not breathe back.

When Paul Flew Away

It was the same as always,
Paul opening the big, black lung
of it with that worried look

while the cats watched
from under the stove,
but when he closed
his eyes and begun to sink
down between the straps
of his bib overalls,
it was like he died. Except
the accordion was still breathing
a waltz between his hands,
except he called back
to us every so often
from wherever he was, "Shit."
Which meant everything
he had ever known
in his life up to that
moment, but this song.
Not some sock-drawer
music of getting a tune out
and then rummaging
for the chord to match,
but together, exactly like
he was breathing the thing
himself. No stomping
either, just Paul twisting
like he was after some deep
itch, only right then
he was starting to lift
out of his chair. Slowly
at first, like flypaper
in a small breeze, then
the whole enormous weight
of him hanging over the sink. God,

he was happy, and I
and the kids was laughing
and happy, when all
at once it come to me,
this is it. Paul is leaving
the old Barcalounger
stuck in second
position, and the TV on top
of the TV that don't
work, and all my hand-paintings
of strawberries as if he never
said this would be Strawberry Farm.
"Hey!" I said out in the yard
because he was already going
right over the roof
of the goat shed, pumping
that song. "What about you
and me?" And Paul
just got farther and smaller
until he looked like a kid
unfolding paper dolls over
and over, or like
he was clapping slowly
at himself, and then
like he was opening up the wings
of some wild, black bird
he had made friends with
just before he disappeared
into the sky above the clouds
all over Maine.

Happiness

Why, Dot asks, stuck in the back
seat of her sister's two-door, her freckled hand
feeling the roof for the right spot
to pull her wide self up onto her left,
the unarthritic, ankle – why
does her sister, coaching outside on her cane,
have to make her laugh so, she flops
back just as she was, though now
looking wistfully out through the restaurant
reflected in her back window, she seems bigger,
and couldn't possibly mean we should go
ahead in without her, she'll be all right, and so
when you finally place the pillow behind her back
and lift her right out into the sunshine,
all four of us are happy, none more
than she, who straightens the blossoms
on her blouse, says how nice it is to get out
once in awhile, and then goes in to eat
with the greatest delicacy (oh
I could never finish all that) and aplomb
the complete roast beef dinner with apple crisp
and ice cream, just a small scoop.

FROM *My Brother Running*

Young Man Going Uphill with a Bird

Going uphill toward her house in snow so deep
the road is gone, the lover walks the tops
of fence posts. Thoughts about his dying child,
or how to keep the farm after the fire
never enter his mind. Not that he's so
preoccupied with balancing himself
in his workboots, but that the deaths of child
and farm haven't yet happened, couldn't happen
on such a luminous night, the gauzy moon
just rising over her father's roof as if
to guide him there. The only howling comes
from her dog, Shep, who has already heard
his lurching steps, and perhaps even smells
the hurt bird he holds in his coat, a gift
he can hardly wait to give. No need to hurry.
Soon, farm boy become impresario,
he'll lift his coat back from the kitchen table
and leave a creature there, dragging its wing.
Soon, cooing softly at its box, she'll shoo
her younger sisters out and shut the door
and draw him close, finding in his grave, dark eyes
how well they've known each other all along.
Soon their long climb together will begin.

The Secret

How have we forgotten her,
the dreamy-faced girl
on this strange evening
at her grandparents' farm?
How have we forgotten
the mad aunt
who rejected her
for having such blue eyes?
Both are difficult to make out
at first, the aunt
standing in twilight
by the kitchen stove,
the niece watching how she stares
and turns to go upstairs
to her room, thinking then
she sees a woman
inside the old woman. And so,
the voices of younger sisters
and neighbor girls coming through
the window from the far
field, she rises
to follow the aunt,
and finding the tall, closed
barrier between them contains
a small keyhole, kneels down
to look right through,
searching she does not know
for what – a secret woman
combing out her hair?

The photograph of a man
placed on a throne
of bureau and doily?
In that door's eye she sees
old repetitious pears across a wall
and, reaching inside the small,
bare bureau to pull
a nightdress out,
her naked aunt,
now turning to show
in the very place where she
herself has just begun
to darken, a gray, matted
and forgotten V. This is the secret
the niece carries into the hall
with old furniture
losing itself in the dusk,
and into her own dim
room with its pattern
vanishing on the wall,
and deep into her brain
where she will never forget
the color that will one day
be her own color.
From some other world
her sisters call and call
her name, which she hardly knows,
lying there with both hands
between her legs, listening
to the shivering trees.

The Life

There is a moment
when the arms,
sent behind you

to locate the sleeves
of your coat, become lost
in the possibility

of the garment lifting
above them. This
is why they thrash

out of your sight,
searching not
for what you think

you want, but what
behind your own back
you long for,

a seamless place
that opens
to another life.

Seeing Mercer, Maine

Beyond the meadow
on Route 2, the semis
go right on by,

48

hauling their long
echoes into the trees.
They want nothing to do
with this road buckling downhill
toward the Grange and Shaw
Library, Open 1–5 P.M. SAT,
and you may wonder
why I've brought you here,
too. It's not SAT,
and apart from summer, the big
event in town's the bog
water staggering down the falls.
Would it matter if I told you
people live here – the old
man from the coast who built
the lobster shack
in a hayfield;
the couple with the sign
that says Cosmetics
and Landfill; the woman
so shy about her enlarged leg
she hangs her clothes
outdoors at night? Walk down this road
awhile. What you see here in daytime –
a kind of darkness that comes
from too much light –
you'll need to adjust
your eyes for. The outsized
hominess of that TV dish,
for instance, leaning
against its cupboard
of clapboard. The rightness

of the lobsterman's shack –
do you find it, tilted
there on the sidehill,
the whitecaps of daisies
just cresting beside it
in the light wind?

Making Things Clean

One would hardly recognize him like this,
the high-school shop teacher, glasses off,
bent over the kitchen sink. Nearby,
house dresses and underpants flutter
in the window of the Maytag he bought
for his mother. Its groaning is the only
sound while she washes his hair,
lifting the trembling water in her hands
as she has always done, working foam up
from his gray locks like the lightest
batter she ever made. Soon enough,
glasses back on, he will stand
before students who mock his dullness;
soon, putting up clothes, she'll feel
the ache of a body surrendering to age.
A little longer let him close his eyes
against soap by her apron, let her move
her fingers slowly, slowly in this way
the two of them have found to be together,
this transfiguring moment in the world's
old work of making things clean.

The One Who Will Save You

If some afternoon you
should pass by there,
and the woman comes out swooping
her blue bathrobe back
from her path and crying, "Baby, oh my
sweet baby," it won't be you
she means, nor you
the hubby wearing motorcycles
on his T-shirt and jumping
down from the stairless
sliding glass door
says he wants to kill, so just
stand still. It's the dog
they'll be after, the shadow
under the not-quite sunk pink
Chevy, ratcheting itself up
with a slow, almost inaudible
growl into the biggest, ugliest
shepherd–Labrador–husky
cross West Central Maine
has ever seen. It won't matter
if the two shirtless fat kids
come from around back with
hubcaps on their heads and shout
even louder than their father does,
"Queenie!" By then Queenie,
less a queen than a chain-
saw lunging at the potential
cordwood of your legs,

won't know or care what
humans have named her. There'll be
no hope for you, Pal, unless
that is, the teenage daughter,
who comes across the front lawn's
dandelions in her tank top
every so often to set me free,
releases you, too – shaking her head
as if only you and she
could see how impossible
her stupid parents and this uncool
dog really are, and lifting it,
like that, by the collar
to create a bug-eyed
sausage that gasps
so loud her mother gasps – not
that the daughter will care. "Mother,"
she'll say, eyeing the sorry choice
of afternoon attire, "you should see
how you look." Then, flicking
Dad out of the way
and renaming the creature
she's created "Peckerwood,"
she'll march as if she
herself were now queen
back through that kingdom
of California raisins and tires
and Christmas lights decking the front
porch in July, and past the screen door
with the sign saying This
Is Not A Door, to disappear,

rump by rump with a bump
and a grind to you,
through the real screen door.

Reading Poems at the Grange Meeting
in What Must Be Heaven

How else to explain that odd,
perfect supper – the burnished
lasagna squares, thick
clusters of baked
beans, cole slaw pink

with beet juice? How else
to tell of fluorescent
lights touching their once-familiar
faces, of pipes branching over
their heads from the warm

furnace-tree, like no tree on earth –
or to define the not-quite
dizziness of going
up the enclosed, turning
stair afterward to find them

in the room of the low
ceiling, dressed as if for play?
Even Dolly Lee, talked into coming
to this town thirty
years ago from California,

wears a blue sash,
leaving each curse against winters
and the black fly far
behind. And beside her
Francis, who once did the talking,

cranking his right hand
even then, no doubt, to jump-
start his idea, here uses his hand
to raise a staff, stone silent,
a different man. For the Grange

meeting has begun, their fun
of marching serious-faced together
down the hall to gather
stout Bertha who bears the flag
carefully ahead of herself

like a full
dust mop, then
marching back again,
the old floor making long
cracking sounds

under their feet like late
pond ice that will not break –
though now the whole group stands
upon it, hands
over their hearts. It does not matter

that the two retarded men, who in the other
world attempted haying for Mrs. Carter,
stand here beside her
pledging allegiance in words
they themselves have never heard.

It does not matter
that the Worthy Master,
the Worthy Overseer
and the Secretary sit back
down at desks

donated by School District
#54 as if all three were
in fifth grade: everyone here
seems younger – the shiny bald-headed
ones, the no longer old

ladies, whose spectacles
fill with light as they
look up, and big Lenny
too, the trucker, holding the spoons
he will play soon

and smiling at me as if
the accident that left
the long cheek scar and mashed
his ear never happened. For I
am rising

with my worn folder
beside the table of potholders,
necklaces made from old newspaper
strips and rugs braided
from rags. It does not matter

that in some narrower time
and place I did not want
to read to them on
Hobby Night. What matters is
that standing in – how else

to understand it – the heaven
of their wonderment,
I share the best
thing I can make – this stitching
together of memory

and heart-scrap, this wish
to hold together Francis,
Dolly Lee, the Grange officers,
the retarded men and everybody
else here levitating

ten feet
above the dark
and cold and regardless
world below them and me
and poetry.

FROM *Talking in the Dark*

This Love Song

He is such an unlikely lover, wearing sneakers
someone has dressed him in, his old
floppy legs hanging down from the bed
they have sold his house for. What he loves
is not even here, and when he rocks
this way, his head thrown back, holding only himself,
he is not much more than a chest
heaving and a few teeth you can almost
see right through. It is the clear refusal
to open his eyes and be where he is
among the pleading nurses and his roommate,
the sad, lost man, that sets him apart.
It is how he will not let go
of all he does not have, making up this song
about it, this love song, which fills
the lonely hall outside his room and no one can stop.

Old Guys

Driving beyond a turn in the mist
of a certain morning, you'll find them
beside a men-at-work sign,
standing around with their caps on
like penguins, all bellies and bills.
They'll be watching what the yellow truck
is doing and how. Old guys know trucks,

59

having spent days on their backs under them
or cars. You've seen the gray face
of the garage mechanic lying on his pallet, old
before his time, and the gray, as he turns
his wrench looking up through the smoke
of his cigarette, around the pupil
of his eye. This comes from concentrating
on things the rest of us refuse
to be bothered with, like the thickening
line of dirt in front of the janitor's
push broom as he goes down the hall, or the same
ten eyelets inspector number four checks
on the shoe, or the box after box
the newspaper man brings to a stop
in the morning dark outside the window
of his car. Becoming expert in such details
is what has made the retired old guy
behind the shopping cart at the discount store
appear so lost. Beside him his large wife,
who's come through poverty and starvation
of feeling, hungry for promises of more
for less, knows just where she is,
and where and who she is sitting by his side
a year or so later in the hospital
as he lies stunned by the failure of his heart
or lung. "Your father" is what she calls him,
wearing her permanent expression
of sadness, and the daughter, obese
and starved herself, calls him "Daddy,"
a child's word, crying for a tenderness
the two of them never knew. Nearby, her husband,

who resembles his father-in-law in spite
of his Elvis sideburns, doesn't say
even to himself what's going on inside him,
only grunts and stares as if the conversation
they were having concerned a missing bolt
or some extra job the higher-ups just gave him
because this is what you do when you're bound,
after an interminable, short life to be an old guy.

Old Cadillacs

Who would have guessed they would end this way,
rubbing shoulders with old Scouts and pickups
at the laundromat, smoothing out frost heaves

all the way home? Once cherished for their style,
they are now valued for use, their back seats
full of kids, dogs steaming their windows; yet this

is the life they have wanted all along, to let go
of their flawless paint jobs and carry cargoes
of laundry and cheap groceries down no-name roads,

wearing bumper stickers that promise Christ
until they can travel no more and take their places
in backyards, far from the heated garages

of the rich who rejected them, among old tires
and appliances and chicken wire, where the poor
keep each one, dreaming, perhaps, of a Cadillac

with parts so perfect it might lift past sixty
as if not touching the earth at all, as if to pass
through the eye of a needle and roll into heaven.

The Puppy

From down the road, starting up
and stopping once more, the sound
of a puppy on a chain who has not yet
discovered he will spend his life there.
Foolish dog, to forget where he is
and wander until he feels the collar
close fast around his throat, then cry
all over again about the little space
in which he finds himself. Soon,
when there is no grass left in it
and he understands it is all he has,
he will snarl and bark whenever
he senses a threat to it.
Who would believe this small
sorrow could lead to such fury
no one would ever come near him?

Trying to Find Her Teeth

This little boy with the taped glasses,
the dreamy kid nobody would put in charge
of details – he is the one I must slip inside
to look up into the toothless, angry face

of my mother whose voice does not come
all the way out of her mouth. Have I forgotten
my lunchbox at school? Is this the day
I lost my paper-route list? What I know
is that standing above me in her red bathrobe
and waving her switch, she is about to ask
if I will ever do it again until I cannot
say no. What I know, tasting salt afterward
in my bed, is that she never got
the brand-new teeth. Did I only dream
she kissed me, father gone, under the lamplight
and told me of the lovely white smile
that would change her life, my life –
or did it happen? Now I am looking up
to find her at the sewing machine again
with only sharp pins between her lips
and in her hands the bright needle moving oh
so quick and deep. Now all her work of shirtsleeves
and pantcuffs is cleared away, and I am singing.
Before me, in the lamplight, a shut-faced man
sits listening in dark lapels. There at his side,
my happy mother, wearing lipstick, cannot stop
smiling at me with somebody else's mouth.

The Book of A

Raised during the Depression, my stepfather
responded to the economic opportunity
of the 1950s by buying more
and more cheap, secondhand things

meant to transform his life.
"I got this for a hundred bucks,"
he said, patting the tractor that listed
to one side, or the dump truck that started
with a roar and wouldn't dump.
Spreading the parts out on his tarp,
he'd make the strange whistle
he said he learned from the birds
for a whole morning
before the silence set in.
Who knows where he picked up
the complete A–Z encyclopedias,
embossed in gold and published
in 1921? "They were going to take these
to the dump," he said. Night after night
he sat up, determined to understand
everything under the sun
worth knowing, and falling asleep
over the book of A. Meanwhile, as the weeks,
then the months passed, the moon
went on rising over the junk machines
in the tall grass of the only
world my stepfather ever knew,
and nobody wrote to classify
his odd, beautiful whistle, formed,
somehow, in the back of his throat
when a new thing seemed just about to happen
and no words he could say expressed his hope.

Weeds

In my fifty-fifth year,
kneeling in my garden
to pull a weed,
I discover my father,
whom I hardly knew,
lying down in his garden.
His heart so damaged now
no doctor would remove
the cataracts that spoil his sight,
he has no other way to see
what he is doing. With him again
in his sad dimness,
I don't want to lecture him
about the smell of booze
or talk about the seed
he left long ago untended.
Aging father with my own
flaws of the heart,
I am content to see him
resting among the carrots
and peas. It is enough
to listen to him sip
the air in the innocence
of his concentration,
doing his best with the weeds.

Waving Goodbye

Why, when we say goodbye
at the end of an evening, do we deny
we are saying it at all, as in We'll
be seeing you, or I'll call, or Stop in,
somebody's always at home? Meanwhile, our friends,
telling us the same things, go on disappearing
beyond the porch light into the space
which except for a moment here or there
is always between us, no matter what we do.
Waving goodbye, of course, is what happens
when the space gets too large
for words – a gesture so innocent
and lonely, it could make a person weep
for days. Think of the hundreds of unknown
voyagers in the old, fluttering newsreel
patting and stroking the growing distance
between their nameless ship and the port
they are leaving, as if to promise I'll always
remember, and just as urgently, Always
remember me. Is it loneliness, too,
that makes the neighbor down the road lift
two fingers up from his steering wheel as he passes
day after day on his way to work in the hello
that turns into goodbye? What can our own raised
fingers do for him, locked in his masculine
purposes and speeding away inside the glass?
How can our waving wipe away the reflex
so deep in the woman next door to smile
and wave on her way into her house with the mail,
we'll never know if she is happy

or sad or lost? It can't. Yet in that moment
before she and all the others and we ourselves
turn back to our disparate lives, how
extraordinary it is that we make this small flag
with our hands to show the closeness we wish for
in spite of what pulls us apart again
and again: the porch light snapping off,
the car picking its way down the road through the dark.

Glass Night

Come, warm rain
and cold snap,
come, car light

and country road
winding me around
dark's finger,

come, flash
of mailbox and sign,
and shine

of brush,
stubble and all
the lit lonely

windows wrapped
in the glass branches
of tree

after flying tree.
Come, moon-coated
snow hills, and flung

far ahead pole
by pole the long
glass cobweb

in my high beam
that carries me deeper.
Come, deeper

and mute dark
and speech of light.
Come, glass night.

The Characters of Dirty Jokes

Two weeks after the saleswoman told the farm brothers
to wear condoms so she wouldn't get pregnant,
they sit on the porch wondering if it's all right
to take them off. They are about as bewildered
as the man at the bar whose head is tiny
because he asked the fairy godmother, granter of all
wishes, for a little head. Except for a moment,
you get the feeling, none of them have been that happy
about being attached to the preposterous requirements
of the things between their legs, which in their resting
state, even the elephant thinks are a scream.
"How do you breathe through that thing?" he asks

the naked man. What the naked man replies, looking down
with this new view of himself, the joke doesn't say,
though he's probably not about to laugh. On the other
hand, what was so funny about our own stories
as boys and girls when we heard our first ones,
suddenly wearing patches of hair that had nothing
to do with Sunday school or math class? How lovely
that just as we were discovering the new distance
between ourselves and polite society, the secret
lives of farm girls and priests were pressed
into our ears. Later, when we found ourselves
underneath house mortgages and kids' dental bills,
having taken up the cause of ideal love, they got funny
because they'd never heard of it, still worried,
say, about penis size, like the guy who had his
lengthened by the addition of a baby elephant's
trunk and was doing fine until the cocktail party
where the hostess passed out peanuts.
Their obsessions revealed at the end of their jokes,
they have always been losers, going back to Richard Nixon,
who tried oral sex but never could get it
down Pat, going all the way back to Eve,
thrown out of the Garden for making the first candy,
Adam's peanut brittle. Yet let us celebrate the characters
of dirty jokes, so like us who have made them
in the pure persistence of their desire,
the innocent wish to find a way out of their bodies.

Poem for My Feet

O feet, when they called me "Beanstalk"
at 14, meaning my body was what suddenly happened
after the planting of magic beans, my arms
startled branches, my head looking down from the sky,
I scarcely heard, stunned as I was by what magic
had done overnight to you. Bad enough I now owned a penis
so unpredictable I had to put books
on it walking down school halls, I had your long
arches and toes which, whatever I put on them, stuck out
all the more. Great pedicles, those first cordovans
were the worst, deep maroon dream shoes
that floated footless on their page in the catalogue
I ordered from, and arrived dead weights
in a huge box, so red and shiny
and durable, their names lasted through two years
of high school: Clodhoppers, Platters, Skis.
And years later, when I took you to dinner parties
where they were too polite to name you
and just stopped talking altogether – when I sat
with legs crossed holding my teacup in that parlor
in Chile and suddenly noticed the small people
seated around me were staring at how the pulse
lifted my big foot as it hung there in front of them,
was I any better off? How could I tell them
that I understood they had all they could do
not to begin crossing themselves right there,
that inside my foot and my outsized body,
I only wanted to be small, too? But peace,
old toe-lifters, if I couldn't accept you then,
if just last month I stood barefoot before my family

and called you in jest my Oscar-Mayer five-packs
wiggling a big toe while singing, as in
the commercial, "I wish I were an Oscar-Mayer wiener,"
forgive the bad joke and the accusations, this
has never been your fault. Unconcerned with fitting in,
all you ever wanted was to take me in the direction
of my own choosing. Never mind the hands
getting all the attention as they wave to others
on the street, this is not their poem,
but only yours, steady vessels, who all along
have resisted my desire to be like everyone else,
who turn after the hands are done and carry me
with resolute steps into my separate life.

The Retarded Children Play Baseball

Never mind the coaches who try
to teach them the game,
and think of the pleasure

of the large-faced boy
on second who raises hand and glove
straight up making the precise

shape of the ball, even though
the ball's now over
the outfield. And think of the left

and right fielders going deeper
just to watch its roundness
materialize out of the sky

and drop at their feet. Both teams
are so in love with this moment
when the bat makes the ball jump

or fly that when it happens
everybody shouts, and the girl
with slanted eyes on first base

leaps off to let the batter by.
Forget the coaches shouting back
about the way the game is played

and consider the game
they're already playing, or playing
perhaps elsewhere on some other field,

like the shortstop, who stands transfixed
all through the action, staring
at what appears to be nothing.

Why We Need Poetry

Everyone else is in bed, it being, after all,
three in the morning, and you can hear
how quiet the house has become each time
you pause in the conversation you are having
with your close friend to take a bite
of your sandwich. Is it getting the wallpaper
around you in the kitchen up at last
that makes cucumbers and white bread, the only

things you could find to eat, taste so good,
or is it the satisfaction of having discovered
a project that could carry the two of you
into this moment made for nobody else?
Either way, you're here in the pleasure
of the tongue, which continues after
you've finished your sandwich, for now
you are savoring the talk alone – how
by staring at the band of fluorescent light
over the sink or the pattern you hadn't
noticed in the wallpaper, you can see
where the sentence you've started, line
by line, should go. Only love could lead you
to think this way, or to care so little
about how you speak, you end up saying
what you care most about exactly right,
each small allusion growing larger
in the light of your friend's eye.
And when the light itself grows larger,
it's not the next day coming through the windows
of that redone kitchen, but you,
changed by your hunger for the words
you listen to and speak, their taste
which you can never get enough of.

Love Handles

If the biker's head where the hair was
shines in the sun while he blows
into his helmet to get the heat out

of it, she doesn't mind. It's not him
with the bald spot, it's just him. And she likes
feeling the fleshy overhang in the front
when she climbs on behind and takes him
into her arms. How else could he carry her
up and up the wild, quick, five-
note scale that they float off on? Anyway,
who doesn't love a belly? Forget the revulsion
we're supposed to feel looking at the before picture
in the diet ad and remember the last time
you asked a good friend you hadn't seen in years,
"What's *this*?" patting where the shirt
stuck out. Or think of feeling somebody's
back, like the two old lovers lying in bed, she
turned away from him inquiring over her shoulder
with her finger, "What's that, right there, is it
a bug bite or a mole?" And he, the one trusted
with this place so private not even she
can see it, touching it, not skin or flesh
in this special, ordinary moment but something
else, something more, like the hand the hunched
old lady has in hers going across the fast-food
parking lot. Beside her an old man, the hand's
owner, is walking with what you and I
might think of as a sort of kick
over and over, but what they don't think of at all,
balancing each other like this so they can arrive
together to get a burger. The point is, you can't
begin to know how to hold another body
in your eye until you've held it a few times
in your hand or in your arms. Any ten couples

at the Fireman's Ball could tell you that. Put aside
your TV dreams of youth running its fingers
over the hood of a new car, or the smiling
faces of Tammy the weather girl and Bob on sports,
she with the unreal hair and he with the hair
that's not real, and imagine the baldies
with their corsaged wives under the whirling
chunks of light at the Ball. Think of their innocence,
all dressed up to be with the ones they've known
half their lives. See how after those years
of nudging and hugging and looking each other all over,
they glide, eyes closed, on love handles across the floor.

FROM *Fire*

How I Became a Poet

"Wanted" was the word I chose
   for him at age eight, drawing the face
of a bad guy with comic-book whiskers,
then showing it to my mother. This was how,

after my father left us, I made her smile
at the same time I told her I missed him,
and how I managed to keep him close by
in that house of perpetual anger,

becoming his accuser and his devoted
accomplice. I learned by writing
to negotiate between what I had,
and that more distant thing I dreamed of.

The Good-Boy Suit

I was four when my mother
stitched herself, working late
at night, my father gone.
She put her hand into the light

of the Singer and pressed
the treadle until the needle
sang through her thumb.
I stood back from the piles

of clothes she sewed afterward
with her bandaged hand,
pins shining in her shut,
angry mouth, gone away herself.

She would not stitch me,
I thought. But I was a bad boy,
and why did my mother say over
and over she would sew me

a new suit if I was good?
I was afraid to be good,
I was afraid not to be good.
My mother switched me.

My mother switched and stitched.
"Turn around," she said, pushing pins
with her bandage into the patterns
on my arms and chest, "Stand still,"

making a tickle when she measured
my inseam. I was the bad boy
who couldn't, who forgot
to flush, who was afraid

to clean out from under the bed
or watch my mother lean
forward putting her hand into
the Singer's light that was like fire

in her eyes and hair.
The good-boy suit just let her

stick pins in it and cut it
and push it into the fire again

and again with her shut face
to stitch it, only the two of them
together in the dark all night long.
So when I came downstairs

to find them, my mother
held up the good-boy suit
that had my arms and chest
and legs. "It's perfect," she said,

smiling at it, and her hand, with no
bandage now, was perfect too.
I was the one who wasn't.
I couldn't answer when my mother

asked me why I did not like
or want the good-boy suit,
or why, even at a time like this,
I had to be such a bad boy.

Shovels

Who could have guessed he would choose
to spend so much of his time bent over
a shovel, one wrist so weak he wore
an ace bandage on it, his asthmatic lungs
forcing him to stop for breath again

and again. "Never mind," he would say to us,
his three young stepsons, when we
stopped too, "get back to work."

                                    Every weekend
for a whole winter, we hauled cinders
from the paper mill to level the driveway.
That next spring he had us digging holes
for the barn's corner posts, angry that we kept
fighting with each other in our anger
about the endlessness of banging our shovels
into the nearly frozen ground. Why did he
drive us that way? Why was he so hard
on himself, always the last one to come
in the house out of the dark.

                                  One summer
we dug until we found ourselves inside
a waist-high trench he said would bring water
up from the river to the plants of his nursery.
"You'll never get anywhere," he told us,
"until you learn the meaning of work."

Above ground in the moonlight, as I return
through this poem, the tall grass has no idea
where we laid that pipe. The sprinkler system
for the nursery, dead for years, has forgotten why.
All the truckloads of fill we brought to prevent
the bank's erosion are on their way down
into the river. In the back of the old barn,
its aluminum siding curled from the weather,
the shovels we once used stand upside-down
against the wall in the window's light like flowers,
making a kind of memorial to the work

we did then, some with blunted points, some
scalloped at the center, where after all those years
of shoveling, they shoveled themselves away.

The One I Think of Now

At the end of my stepfather's life
when his anger was gone,
and the saplings of his failed
nursery had grown into trees,
my newly feminist mother had him
in the kitchen to pay for all
those years he only did the carving.
"You know where that is,"
she would say as he looked
for a knife to cut the cheese
and a tray to serve it with,
his apron wide as a dress
above his work boots, confused
as a girl. He is the one I think of now,
lifting the tray for my family,
the guests, until at last he comes
to me. And I, no less confused,
look down from his hurt eyes as if
there were nothing between us
except an arrangement of cheese,
and not this bafflement, these
almost tender hands that once
swung hammers and drove machines
and insisted that I learn to be a man.

Sleep

The young dog would like to know
why we sit so long in one place
intent on a box that makes the same
noises and has no smell whatever.
"Get out! Get out!" we tell him
when he asks us by licking the back
of our hand, which has small hairs,
almost like his. Other times he finds us
motionless with papers in our lap
or at a desk looking into a humming
square of light. Soon the dog understands
we are not looking, exactly, but sleeping
with our eyes open, then goes to sleep
himself. Is it us he cries out to,
moving his legs somewhere beyond
the rooms where we spend our lives?
We don't think to ask, upset
as we are in the end with the dog,
who has begun throwing the old,
shabby coat of himself down on every
floor or rug in the apartment. "Sleep,"
we say, "all that damn dog does is sleep."

Voiceless

The swelling
that starts under the eye
of the mother rising

for third shift, then
turns into a welt.

The ill man's hand
on the banister
as he climbs step
by step listening
to his quickening heart.

The silence of cats
watching the old woman
in a bathrobe explain to them
how everyone loved her
in the red dress.

The bowed head
of the son in the chair
too afraid to tell
his certain, angry father
he is not to blame.

The still chest of the wife
who has learned
not to have feelings
so her vigilant husband
will not know them.

The face nobody sees
on the glass door
of the cooler, not even
the one who opens it to stock
cases, night after night.

Speech

All along, he wants us to know,
the simple solution he offers
has been right there, obvious

as his open palm. No wonder
he seems a little angry with us,
who have spent our time shrugging

our shoulders or teetering our right
hands back and forth, while he's
found this truth that makes right

and wrong perfectly divisible.
Does our doubt return
because of the loneliness

we sense in him, forming precise
compartments with his hands
at the lectern inside his small

beam of light? Or is it the absence
in his speech of an expression for two
things at once no language

seems complete without: *mas o menos,*
comme ci, comme ça, or that
stubborn, beautiful word *though.*

An Executive's Afterlife

The others in hell can't believe he's allowed
to go free for eternity. Part of their punishment
as they sit beside the fire in chains is to watch him
pass by. His punishment, after a life of having all
the answers, is to have none whatsoever and keep
bumping into people who ask him questions:
his wife, for instance, here because she never dared
ask him any, choosing to die a slow death instead.
How are you? is all she has to say to make him turn,
always for the first time, to discover her with no
coiffure and ashes on her face. Under his hand,
which never leaves his chest, the pain feels like
the beginnings of the coronary that killed him,
and it only gets worse when he sees the son he bullied,
an old man in chains. Unable to leave the comfort
of his father's wealth and live his own life, rich
or poor, the son now kneels at the flames trying
to get warm, with no result, forever. He's too intent
to ask his question, which the father, on his way,
already knows: *Why did you do this?* Soon he walks
past former doormen, bellhops, and bag ladies
who can't wait to ask him the one thing that makes
their day, even in hell: *Who do you think you are?*
Nobody's nice, except the stewardess from first-class.
She liked serving passengers with expensive suits
and wristwatches so much, she must seek them out
with her eternally nice smile to inquire, *Would you
like something to drink?* She has no drinks,
of course, this is hell, after all, so he's left to suffer

his unquenchable thirst, not a hurt or absence
he feels in the throat, but there under his hand,
in his sensitive and innocent heart, which the devil,
to give him his due, went nearly to heaven to find.

Smoking

Once, when cigarettes meant pleasure
instead of death, before Bogart
got lung cancer and Bacall's
voice, called "smoky," fell

into the gravel of a lower octave,
people went to the movies just
to watch the two of them smoke.
Life was nothing but a job,

Bogart's face told us, expressionless
except for the recurrent grimace,
then it lit up with the fire
he held in his hands and breathed

into himself with pure enjoyment
until each word he spoke afterward
had its own tail of smoke.
When he offered a cigarette

to Bacall, she looked right at him,
took it into her elegant mouth
and inhaled, while its smoke curled
and tangled with his. After the show,

just to let their hearts race and taste
what they'd seen for themselves,
the audiences felt in purses,
shirt pockets, and even inside

the sleeves of T-shirts, where packs
of cigarettes were folded, by a method
now largely forgotten. "Got a light?"
somebody would say, "Could I bum

one of yours?" never thinking
that two of the questions most
asked by Americans everywhere
would undo themselves and disappear

like the smoke that rose
between their upturned fingers,
unwanted in a new nation
of smoke-free movie theaters,

malls and restaurants, where politicians
in every state take moral positions
against cigarettes so they can tax them
for their favorite projects. Just fifty years

after Bogart and Bacall, smoking
is mostly left in the hands of waitresses
huddled outside fancy inns, or old
clerks on the night shift in mini-marts,

or hard-hats from the road crew
on a coffee-break around the battered

tailgate of a sand truck – all paying
on installment with every drag

for bridges and schools. Yet who else
but these, who understand tomorrow
is only more debt, and know
better than Bogart that life is work,

should be trusted with this pleasure
of the tingling breath they take today,
these cigarettes they bum and fondle,
calling them affectionate names

like "weeds" and "cancer sticks," holding
smoke and fire between their fingers
more casually than Humphrey Bogart
and blowing it into death's eye.

History of Talking on the Phone

Once the phone, called the "telephone,"
was a voice one heard by pressing
what looked like a stethoscope
to one's ear, answering by shouting
at a device on the wall.

This was before talking on the phone
was invented – a more intimate exchange
using a receiver that allowed one to speak
to the voice while holding it in the hand.

Everyone held it and spoke to it.

In stereoscope movies of the period, starlets
lounged on beds talking on the phone
as they stroked its long cord. Men in high-rise
offices commanded, "Put her through!"

or sat in bedrooms on a split screen
talking on phones that matched their pajamas.

In the small towns of America, the tender gesture
of hunching one shoulder to talk on the phone
became popular with housewives washing dishes

and men in the workplace, whose big shoulders
balancing the voice as they smiled and talked to it

while turning the pages of a parts catalogue
or toweling grease from their hands
made a poignant moment
in the history of talking on the phone.

In the cities, meanwhile, where phones
had begun to resemble miniature
PC keyboards, so square and flat
not even teenagers practicing on private lines
in their rooms could balance them,

talking on the phone rapidly advanced
to contacting someone by phone,
or explaining what one wanted into a machine.

The voice, now a filed message,
was what one listened to all alone,

like the starlet in the movie
coming home all smiles after a week away
to the ominous dark of her apartment
and releasing voices

until she gets to the one
she can hardly believe and plays it

over and over, unable to stop crying.

What Became

What became of the dear
strands of hair pressed
against the perspiration
of your lover's brow
after lovemaking as you gazed
into the world of those eyes,
now only yours?

What became of any afternoon
that was so vivid you forgot
the present was up to its old
trick of pretending
it would be there
always?

What became of the one
who believed so deeply
in this moment he memorized
everything in it and left
it for you?

The Rules of the New Car

After I got married and became
the stepfather of two children, just before
we had two more, I bought it, the bright
blue sorrowful car that slowly turned
to scratches and the flat black spots
of gum in the seats and stains impossible
to remove from the floor mats. "Never again,"
I said as our kids, four of them by now,
climbed into the new car. "This time,
there will be rules." The first to go
was the rule I made for myself about
cleaning it once a week, though why,
I shouted at the kids in the rearview mirror,
should I have to clean it if they would just
remember to fold their hands. Three years
later, it was the same car I had before,
except for the dent my wife put in the grille
when, ignoring the regulation about snacks,
she reached for a bag of chips on her way
home from work and hit a tow truck. Oh,
the ache I felt for the broken rules,
and the beautiful car that had been lost,

and the car that we now had, on soft
shocks in the driveway, still unpaid for.
Then one day, for no particular reason except
that the car was loaded down with wood
for the fireplace at my in-laws' camp
and groceries and sheets and clothes
for the week, my wife in the passenger seat,
the dog lightly panting beside the kids in the back,
all innocent anticipation, waiting for me
to join them, I opened the door to my life.

Goodbye to the Old Life

Goodbye to the old life,
to the sadness of rooms
where my family slept as I sat

late at night on my island
of light among papers.
Goodbye to the papers

and to the school for the rich
where I drove them, dressed up
in a tie to declare who I was.

Goodbye to all the ties
and to the life I lost
by declaring, and a fond goodbye

to the two junk cars that lurched
and banged through the campus
making sure I would never fit in.

Goodbye to the finest campus
money could buy, and one
final goodbye to the paycheck

that was always gone
before I got it home.
Farewell to the home,

and a heartfelt goodbye
to all the tenants who rented
the upstairs apartment,

particularly Mrs. Doucette,
whose washer overflowed
down the walls of our bathroom

every other week, and Mr. Green,
determined in spite of the evidence
to learn the electric guitar.

And to you there, the young man
on the roof turning the antenna
and trying not to look down

on how far love has taken you,
and to the faithful wife
in the downstairs window

shouting, "That's as good
as we're going to get it,"
and to the four hopeful children

staying with the whole program
despite the rolling picture
and the snow – goodbye,

wealth and joy to us all
in the new life, goodbye!

Charles by Accident

Named Charlie for the relaxed
companionship we expected,
he became Charles for his butler-like
obedience, though he went off-duty

the morning my wife walked back
from the mailbox watching him toss
what looked like a red sock
gloriously into the air,

seeing it was actually the cardinal
she had been feeding all winter.
Why did she scream like that
was the question his whole,

horrified body seemed to ask, just
before he disappeared, back soon

at the door, black coat, white collar,
all ready to serve us: who was

that other dog, anyway? Who,
on the other hand, was this one,
chosen at the pound for his breed
and small size, now grown into three

or four different kinds of large
dogs stuck together. It wasn't his fault,
of course, that in the end he wasn't
Charlie, or even, considering the way

he barked at guests and sniffed them,
Charles exactly. Besides, it couldn't
have been easy to be whatever
sort of dog he was. Part retriever,

he spent his winters biting ice,
and summers dirt out of his tufted paws.
Part Collie, all he ever got to herd
were two faux sheep: a wire-haired terrier

that bit him back and a cat that turned
and ran up trees. An accidental sheep-dog,
Charles by accident, and our dog only
after he'd been disowned, he understood

that life is all missed connections
and Plan B – the reason why, perhaps,
no one could quite pat him or say
good boy enough, and why sometimes,

asleep, he mourned, working his legs
as if running to a place he could never
reach, beyond Charles or any other
way we could think of to call him.

Driving North in Winter

All the way to Mercer these
rooms left out
in the dark –

lamplight and two chairs
the old couple sit
reading in,

a table where a family
comes together
for dinner –

the rest of the houses, one
with the night. How
blessed they are,

the man hanging his ordinary
coat in the small world
of a kitchen,

the woman turning to her cupboard,
both of them held
from the cold

and the vastness by nothing
but trusting
inattention

and one beam of light,
like us passing by
in the darkness,

you napping, me wide awake
and grateful for this
moment

we've also been given, apart
in our way of being
together, living

in the light.

FROM *The Ghosts of You and Me*

My Father Going Away

In a room far back in my mind
with strangers, my father
pressed the thick rim

of the glass to my mouth
burning my lips and throat,
then went back up

to where the laughter was.
My father was always
going away. "Where are you?"

I asked the tiny holes
in the phone my mother
handed me, unable to fit

his answer to my ear.
I spoke to my father
after he left us again

and again. Once, years
later, he was there,
wearing the odd, worn face

his real life had happened to,
and I, at the door of the present,
standing in the past. "I can't

hear you," I told him.
He was the slurred voice
that talked to itself

in a rental car while I
drove him through
the night to the city

where he would leave me
for the last time. Who were
the strangers that laughed

and drank with my father
in the house at the end
of the dark? All dead now,

and my father himself now dead,
but not before he twists
a twenty into my hand

next morning with his shaking
hand so hard I feel it
burning as I board the train.

Outside my father going away
is waving and shouting
something that makes him

start toward me, something
he has held back all this time
behind the glass.

The Boy Carrying the Flag

Once, as the teenage boy marched up
and down the gutter with the wide blade
of a shovel above his head, and the goats
turned toward him in their stalls
undoing with their blats the band
music he held in his mind,

his stepfather, who had only asked,
for Christ's sake, to have the barn
cleaned out, rested his hand
on his hip in the doorway.
The boy would not have guessed
when he marched in his first parade

that he carried the flag for his stepfather,
or for his angry mother, also raised
for work and self-denial
during the Depression. Seeing him
dressed up like that to leave her stuck
on a failing farm with chores

as she had been stuck when she was just
his age, his mother remembered he forgot
to feed the chickens and refused
to drive him to the football game.
The old barns and dead cornfields
along the road in the sunless cold

had never seen a hitchhiker in red
wearing spats and lifting a white-

gloved thumb. Everyone stared
from the cars that passed him by,
and when at last he jumped down
from the door of a semi, the whole

marching band waiting in formation
by the buckling steps of the school
and Mr. Paskevitch, whose hands
twitched worse than ever, watched him
walk across the lawn looking
down at his size-fourteen black shoes.

Just one year from now, Paskevitch
would suffer a nervous breakdown
he would never return from,
but today, he raised the baton
to begin the only thing on earth
that could steady his hands, and the boy,

taller than the others, took his position
in the color guard to carry the flag
for Paskevitch, and for the sergeant-
at-arms, Pete LaRoche, so upset
by the hold-up he was screaming
his commands. For this first parade

belonged to LaRoche, too, and to O'Neill,
another son of immigrants, hoisting
the school colors, and to the rifle-bearers,
Wirkkala and Turco, the fat kid
who squinted helplessly against the wind.
Marching with a shuffle, Turco was already

resigned to his life in the shoe shop,
but this was before he went to work
on the night shift and drank all day,
and before Ann Riley, the head majorette
following the boy past the stopped
traffic kicking up her lovely legs,

got pregnant by the quarterback
and was forced to drop out
of the senior class. In this moment
of possibility in the unforgiving 1950s,
she wore nobody's ring around
her neck, and the boy imagined

how easily she had forgiven him
his lateness and the times his mind
wandered and he fell out of step.
For in his secret heart he carried
the flag for Ann as he marched onto
the football field, leaving the town

with its three factories and wasted
farms far behind. There were LaRoche's
and O'Neill's mothers, on their day off
from the flock mill, and there
were the fathers in their shop pants,
and the classmates in school jackets,

and the teachers who looked strange
without their ties, all applauding
and shouting while the band, capped,
plumed, and lifting up the shining bells

of their instruments, marched by –
all here on this dark and windy day

to watch the quarterback, Joe Costello,
Ann's lover-to-be, lead them into the sun,
as were the band and the tallest boy
in the color guard himself,
carrying the stars and stripes
for everyone who was here

and not here in this broken town,
and for their hope in the uncertain
promise that struggled
against his hand as he marched
to his place in the bleachers
among these, his fellow Americans.

Kuhre's Farm

Oh where is the oval mirror that held
each face above the wash basin
in the great kitchen, and where are the faces

of Rick, the hired man with no teeth
who drew the long, black comb
out of his overalls, proud of his hair,
and Andrew, the big, gentle son, who stooped
at the mirror and all the doorways

of that house, and his father, old Kuhre,
leaning on one crutch to watch himself

pass the washcloth slowly across the eyeless
right side of his face? And what
has happened to the room we entered then

to fold our hands before the covered
dishes and gravy boats of the last
dinners at noon in Cornish, New Hampshire,

while Kuhre's aged bride-by-mail
from the old country, who had left him
long ago for the risen Christ, spoke words
half in Danish for Him only,

and the old man seated at my left, stared
straight ahead with the eye he did not have,
eerily there and not there? Each day

on Kuhre's farm the cows walked slowly
out to the fields in their dream
of going out to the fields, and each night
they dreamed of me waving my skinny arms

calling them back to the whitewashed,
cobwebby barn, as I call them now,
latching them in their long row of stalls
where they bawl for grain, and the tangled
barn cats cry for milk, and the milking machine
begins its great breathing and sighing

in the twilight. Here, inside that breathing,
is the window where I watch a black
Buick roll to a stop in the driveway

tipping its chrome teeth into the dust,
here is Les, the town man, slipping
once more through the door that leads
to the second floor and Andrew's wife

while Andrew sits and strokes the udders
of cows to strip them clean,

here are the three of them on the night
I'm asked upstairs, Les in his Hawaiian
shirt with Maggie on the couch, Andrew
by himself in overalls watching packs
of cigarettes with women's legs
dance in the blue light of the TV.

Oh on all my other nights I traveled
to another country, taking the washcloth
from its nail by the mirror above
the kitchen's basin as if taking a ticket

at a station window from my own ghost face,
and passing then to the dining room
with the lamp on the table to fold my hands
in the half-light beside the old woman
going away into the arms of Christ
and the stroke-bound man with one eye
gouged out by the horn of a cow. Yet

each day Kuhre went on walking step
by step, twisting himself between his crutches,
toward me as I pulled on the flywheel

of his ancient tractor until it began its chug-
chug-chug, shaking the ground, shaking
the raised cutter bar, shaking him
as he climbed slowly up its side and lay
his crutches carefully across the gear shift

and took the knob and held it fast, though it
shook in his knuckled hand. Kuhre held us all,

the old woman, the big son with the wife
who longed for a man from town,
and me, the boy raking the cut grass
while he circled me on his tractor, eye side

and eyeless side, though I hoped for rain,
and tuned my radio each night in my bed
until its lit eye opened and a voice
longing for love sang in the darkness.

Oh I am held still inside a silo in that place
of love promised and work going on,
treading and treading in the green rain
of silage that fell from a high window forever
before the time came

when Kuhre himself fell down, losing his hold
on the tractor in one quick stroke,

and Andrew's wife ran away
from the house with the covered dishes
and the oval mirror and the faces now gone,

and I, who dreamed of being free,
was set free from the silo, and from
the endless day after day in the lost fields
of Kuhre's farm, entering then my own life
of work and love and longing.

It

Don't fall for it.
Don't scratch it.
Don't spoil it for everyone else.
Don't take it for granted.

It's not anything to play with.
It's not the end of the world.
It's not brain surgery.
That's not it.

I used to have cravings for it.
It's the last thing I need right now.
I wish it would just go away.
I can't take it anymore.

Why is it so important to you?
Why did you laugh about it?
Why can't you just be quiet about it?
Is it all about you?

It's all sticky.
It's giving me the creeps.

It's worse than I thought.
You're getting it all over yourself.

This is no place for it.
There's no excuse for it.
Take it outside.
Get over it.

Hymn to the Comb-Over

How the thickest of them erupt just
above the ear, cresting in waves so stiff
no wind can move them. Let us praise them
in all of their varieties, some skinny
as the bands of headphones, some rising
from a part that extends halfway around
the head, others four or five strings
stretched so taut the scalp resembles
a musical instrument. Let us praise the sprays
that hold them, and the combs that coax
such abundance to the front of the head
in the mirror, the combers entirely forget
the back. And let us celebrate the combers,
who address the old sorrow of time's passing
day after day, bringing out of the barrenness
of mid-life this ridiculous and wonderful
harvest, no wishful flag of hope but, thick
or thin, the flag itself, unfurled for us all
in subways, offices and malls across America.

The Gangsters of Old Movies

The cars they stole looked as square
as the small-town chumps
who owned them, like a kind of house
with a step in front of the door

and two rooms inside that had couches
and vases for flowers between
the windows. Automobiles,
they were called, the name

of what it felt like for some sap
and his family to sit still
while their overstuffed seats
moved down the street

as if by themselves. Floor it,
said the gangsters of old movies,
squealing their tires, which had nothing
to do with pretty flowers or going

to grandmother's house. So what
if the little thug on the running board
with the heater fell off right in front
of the cops, they were on their way

to the hideout to split the take.
The gangsters of old movies
were in love with motion,
which was why, among the others

who saved their cars in garages
for Sunday drives, they never fit in,
and why, when they entered the bank
to find the place as still

as a lending library or a museum
where all the dough was kept
behind glass, they felt like
shooting holes in the ceiling

and getting the tellers and the bank
president out from behind the bars
to roll around in the lobby and beg
for their lives. How could they explain

to these hopeless throwbacks
to another century that life
was about the pleasures of money
and screwing people out of it

with the engine running,
not quite knowing they belonged
in another century themselves?
Never mind that the little thug

who was always nervous
about making it to the big time
finally sings like a canary to put them
behind bars, too, and forget

the canned lecture on upholding the law
in the last reel that sounds

like a civics lesson by an old maid
in a one-room school,

and rewind to the getaway scene
of the largest heist in history,
where the Boss, in a back seat
with the life savings of all the pigeons

in the heartland tucked away
in his suitcase, sits as unfazed
as a CEO off for the holidays.
See how, in the perfect meeting

of speed and greed, their black cars
hit the main street among sirens
with the authority of a presidential
motorcade. Look again

at how easily they ditch the cops
and turn their square automobiles
into spirals of dust, on the road
to the Future of Our Country.

The 1950s

"Let's take the car after school," the two girls
    would say, which meant they wanted to be taken
    by it, the top down, the wind surfing over
    the wrap-around window. The stepdaughter,

Carol, always drove, just as her new stepfather
insisted, and while her girlfriend Debbie listened
for the lighter to pop out from the dash,
and with its tiny, interior hotplate lit menthol

cigarettes one by one for both of them, they thought
about how the boys would admire them.
When they drove into their station at the A&W
and Carol unhooked the mic to order their Cokes,

pushing back her shoulder-length hair to reveal
her long throat, she thought she resembled
a popular singer. "Beautiful" was the word
the boys used to describe the car as they gathered

around it, stroking its curves and sometimes
asking if they could see what was under
the hood. Then they looked into Carol's amazing
and frightening blue eyes, or Debbie's warm,

compliant ones, the door or fender giving them a way
to steady themselves. All of that was OK
with the stepfather, who required only that they let
no boys inside, or they could never borrow

the car again. Handsome like a man, he really wasn't
much more than a boy himself, and not wanting to be
anyone's father, told them to call him "Petey."
As he said goodbye in his T-shirt some afternoons,

leaning comfortably into the open window of his new
Chevy convertible, he would call Debbie
"Ginger Snap," and his stepdaughter, his favorite,
with a knowing wink, "Angel Pie." He was proud

of the sinuous Hawaiian woman in green he wore
on his muscular forearm and the darker tattoo
in cursive letters of his own name underneath, the same
tattoo he had his new wife ink on the inside

of her ankle. "Don't you go changing on me,"
he would say with a smile before they headed out
the driveway and the motion rose in their ears, but
the two in the car were already changing, Debbie,

who hoped each day at the A&W for a certain
cute boy to return her gaze, and Carol, in distress
because she couldn't quite get the muscular forearm
and the wink out of her mind even after she touched

her cigarette to the lighter and took a deep
drag and tried to find a good station on the radio.

The Last Black and White TV

Were your parents, or you yourself
among those children who left their primitive
games of giant steps and hopscotch to gather
like stunned pygmies before cowboys
and puppets moving in the light of the first

black and white T V s, square bulbs so heavy
it took two men to deliver them? As night
came on in suburban neighborhoods
perhaps like yours, families unfolded
the legs of dinner trays, longing

to be in the studio audience with the host
of the variety show, or in the white kitchen
with the mother and her children as the father
arrived at the right moment in his dark suit
with the knowledge the rest of them craved.

"It needs more contrast," someone would say,
adjusting a knob until the vegetable slicer
they saw between programs or the black and white
shoes or the kitchen range with the glow-clock
in the changing world behind the glass

looked real, then bought the slicer, the shoes,
the kitchen range, and even the new T V
that their old T V said would make them feel
like they were there. This was how the first
black and white T V s made their way

to the homes of the poor, who loved them best,
turning from disappointment all day long
to watch people opening the doors of ranges
and cars, or men with easy-going smiles
give them away on game shows. When they kicked

their sets or pounded them, it was mostly
because the picture was starting to roll

and ruin the happy ending they were so anxious
to see. The last black and white TV might have been
one of these, its console scarred by fists,

flipping scenes of game show contestants
and sheriffs bringing justice to Americans long ago
in the West out of sight again and again.
Or it may have been the set that played itself to death
above the heads of old folks at the nursing home

in the suburbs, grown sick of wonder and desire.
Or perhaps it stares by the old color set into the dust
of your own attic among things you once discovered
on the screen and would hardly imagine longing for,
they are so strange, so useless, and so still.

If You Had Come

If you had come into that room
after her stroke to find
my mother-in-law Sue Reed
and me, our heads bent
toward each other, making faces

so her face would remember
what it had forgot
of the expressions for surprise
and dismay, or if
you had come in the moment

I tried to teach her lips
by forming small lips
and making them breathe,
first to the left, then
to the right of my nose

until she began to laugh,
and laugh because she couldn't
on one side, and both
of us laughed, you might
have imagined what we did

had less to do with instruction
or sorrow than the antics
of lovers, she giving me
her hand then, I taking it
in mine to stroke it

over and over in the pleasure
of being together in the room
where you might have come
to imagine the two of us
together, just as we were.

As Long As We Remember Him He Will Never Die

they said, which explained
why he ended up beside his wife
at the funeral home, not a presence
with a suit and wristwatch,

but a kind of feeling she had.
Others had it too,
so in the days after the funeral,
he would find himself

going down the thruway
in the back seat with his co-workers
from the car pool, or driving
out of the parking lot

at the supermarket, where
days after he was in the ground,
his neighbor swore she saw him.
Getting behind the wheel again

or sitting at breakfast
with his daughter as she recalled
how many sugars he used
in his coffee seemed

too good to be true, because
it wasn't exactly, he being absent
as the space on the bed
his wife reached for,

drawing him to her in this way
that made him immaterial.
Besides, he wasn't there
any longer than it took them

to return to the relentless
motion and change they lived for.

So after he came back
and discovered the counselor

handing his wife a box of tissues
while urging her to put
the past behind her
and move on, and after

he hovered in frustration
above the grandson who tried
to recall him from
the photograph in the album,

and after hearing the conversation
of a man asking whatever happened
to him, and another man
answering, "He's dead,"

he was ready to die
his second death, as he did,
released piece by piece
from each memory until at last

he was gone to that place
where, like them, you and I also
would have been afraid
all that time to lose him,

beyond motion and recalling
and forgetting.

Mistakes About Heaven

1.

Contrary to what is said,
longing exists there.
Imagine the soul as one
so involved with the music
as it played the game
of walking around the chairs,
it discovered too late
that it had no chair. Having lived
its only life in the body,
it sometimes misses
the walking and the sitting down
and above all, the music.

2.

Having done bad things
can actually get you in,
particularly if you have been
a parent, and did bad things
for the love of your children.

3.

Swearing is perfectly okay there,
even though it's hardly practiced,
cursing being a response
to frustrations on earth
that stand in the way
of mortal service. These God damns
every time He is asked.

4.

The ones who deny themselves
all enjoyment in preparation
for heaven gain admission
only because God
feels sorry for them.
There is pleasure in heaven.
God is known
for the way He parties.

5.

Since the basest
of human motivations
are storing up wealth
beyond measure
and plotting for one's own
future, as the sermon
recommends, they have no
honor in heaven.

6.

The holiest are not the men
who once looked upward
in suits or robes
to speak to a ghost,
but the forgotten ones
who sat beside trash barrels
or beneath an overpass
listening to voices,
unsure of which to follow.
Heaven is not up

or down but a place outside
programs. Those most
ready for it have spent
their lives unable
to make up their minds.

7.

Mysteries are not solved.
The most heavenly experience
is the feeling, as in art,
of something immanent
that never quite
takes place. This is the feeling
those who go there
inhabit always.

My Mother Enters Heaven

She is pleased they had the sense
to choose her, and arriving here at last
beside her husband, the one she's spent
the final years of her life proving wrong,

is just what she dreamed of for herself
those long afternoons working in the nursery
he cursed for all the money it lost. "I spent
all my time propagating that forsythia

you discovered, and even got it into
a catalogue," she tells him, speaking the words

she imagines each time she lifted
the spout of her watering can to her pots

inside the tumbledown plastic hut,
her unsold shrubs tangled across the paths
outside. So why does Paul just stand there
balancing that thin, sparking aureole

above his head and gone away in his eye
as if he is alive somewhere, just not here?
If she were back on earth in the spring
she was just taken from, she would pluck off

a twig bearing the delicate yellow flower
and place it in his hand to take away
that expression of longsuffering
and make him pay attention to how good

she has been and how well everything
turned out, even though she had to sell off
the two main growing fields. But Paul's hand,
which she hasn't touched since years before

the junk car he lay down underneath
to undo the transmission rolled off
its blocks and killed him – the hand
just dangles there all creepy and dead

to her. It is so quiet here, she begins
to think all over again about the fight
they had, their worst, on the evening
she found him, how Paul kicked the dirt

in the greenhouse and cursed it, then
cursed her for binding him to it,
and afterward how quiet it was around her
in that place, too, until at last she walked

out by the barn to the source of the silence,
which was the dropped car, and beneath it
his upturned hand, open in welcome
as if to taunt her. All she wanted then

was to flee the hand, but now, standing
in the light of all things made clear,
she holds it and rubs it, wanting only for Paul
to come back free of this halo and the peace

beyond human understanding and understand.
It is in this moment the sparking begins to form
above her own face shining with tears,
and his hand in hers, my mother enters heaven.

The Man He Turned Into

All he wanted was companionship
for his journey and a chair to sit in
while he held his pen and gazed
at his shape-shifting friends,
the clouds, so how has he ended up

with a wife and four children
driving down the highway, his gas
almost gone, holding a steering wheel

that shakes in his hands? What's out
of balance is not only the front end

of his car, but the ratio of his bills
to the pay he gets for teaching English
in high school and, during summers,
mixing milk shakes, house paint,
or cement, which is why,

rather than clouds, he is gazing
at the warning level on his fuel gauge,
hoping this car with bad alignment
and the great harelip the accident
has made in the chrome mouth

of its grille will get him home.
He is, after all, just four miles away
now that he's stopped at the post office
for the mail, done with a day he only
wants to forget, and would have forgotten

except for the envelope that sticks out
from among the bills and second bills
on the passenger seat, returned
from the editor he sent his poem to.
It will only cause disruption if he opens it

to find his poem hasn't been accepted,
and even if the poem has, he could
turn into a twenty-eight year old man
with trembling hands who screams
and weeps above the whine

of scalloped tires that in his broken-
down life he has found a form at last,
the very man he finally does turn into
when he opens it.

That Nothing

In the moment
of your giving up,
the lost keys suddenly
meeting your eyes
from the only place
you could have put them.

The forgotten table
and open book and empty
chair waiting for you
all this time
in the light left on.

A shade lifted
by your loved one
waking upstairs,
the sound
you did not know
you listened for.

The mysterious
penmanship of snow
the branches of a tree

have brought you
standing at your own door.

Nothing ever happens here.
That nothing.

As I Am

Behind my false beard
and the frown line between
the eyebrows I have developed

by trying to pay attention
to the world, I am the same kid
who could never remember

his library books or what
he had been sent to the store for.
"Fog" was the name my teachers

gave to where I spent my time,
a haze that even today
can descend while I'm having

a conversation, or suddenly lift,
revealing the wrong
landmarks drifting past me

on the wrong road I took ten
miles ago. God, it has been lonely
to turn up all those years

where everyone else has arrived
long since. Yet how, without
looking just beyond

the shoulders of others
as they spoke, or searching
everywhere for the pen

I found in my own hand,
could I concentrate on the thought
I learned to write down

at last, back from the place
that has wanted me off-course
and bewildered, just as I am.

My Town

Where it belongs on the state
tourist map, well above the red lobster
on the coast and in between the man
skiing down the slope and the shining dome
of the capitol building, you'll find nothing
except a moose standing in the grass.
But who would come to this place

to see the three-foot long spotted
yellow butterflies faithfully displayed
on the side of LaFlamme's house, or gather
with the others in the Grange Hall to hear

Ethel Chadwick recite with a lisp
and the dazed, oddly beautiful look
in her eye "The Cremation of Sam McGee"

in its entirety on Old Home Day?
Anyway, what (as people from the city
might say after straying off Route 2
to find our few houses thrown downhill
among the trees) do they do here
for work? Nothing important, as you might
guess from how early in the morning

they start up the hill to do it, driving
to the shoe shop two towns over,
or the paper mill, or just down the road
to the store, where Betty DeCarlo stands all
day at the counter asking the same question:
"Can I help you?" I'm the one waiting
in line behind the couple with the skis

on their minivan who don't even notice her alert,
genuine eyes, on their way through Eyeblink,
Maine, to someplace they've heard of,
and I'm the one lying awake listening
to the cars struggling up our hill in the darkness
of 5 A.M. to start their long day,
and at twilight sitting down in the old parlor

with the Redlevskis, that's me, with a bag
of rhubarb I've just picked from my garden
for the two of them. On the television

in the corner a frowning man, on mute,
mimes all the news of concern to the nation.
Meanwhile, they are talking about how good
it is to eat fresh sticks of rhubarb raw, a concern

so small you wouldn't care much about it
unless you could be there to see the face
she makes for the taste, a mixture of sorrow
and pleasure that seems to have her whole life
in it, and to hear, in the lamplight, the intimate
twang of their voices telling me this news
at evening in my town, as I'm telling it

to you now, in this only other place I know
where unexpected things can happen, off the map.

Love Poem

In the beautiful double light of the pond,
our day together has seemed more
than a single day, and now the sunset
clouds of the pond's second sky stretch
all the way from our dock chairs

to Lucy Point, which had no name
until Lucy, Bob and Rita's dog, began
swimming ahead of them to reach it.
Imagine that the pond, which gradually
deepens the red of our sky, remembers

another sky, where the three of them
swim together for the first time,
unaware of the likeness beneath them.
Imagine this is the pond taking them in
with the wide, unblinking eye of its

perpetual knowing and remembering,
where all the days are one day. Here
is the loon that left behind the small, white
after-image of its breast, here above a brown
shadow is the beaver slowly moving

its nose-print. Around it is a darkening
twilight like ours, decades ago, when
the ghost of Harland Hutchinson,
on the roof of the pond's original camp,
brings his hammer down in silence

making the delayed echo of each blow,
which is the pond listening and storing
the sound away in its pond mind. There,
my love, if you can imagine, it is always
twilight, and always the morning after

the hard freeze, when long-dead Caroline
Barlach, up from New York City to winter
in her godforsaken shack and write the great
American novel, bends toward the hole
she has cut in the ice for water to create,

unknown to her, a shaggy, unforgettable
cameo of her face. For nothing in the quick
double-knowing of the pond is ever lost,
though on this night as the wind comes up,
the single cry of a loon falls away

somewhere beyond Lucy Point,
and the reflection of the pines that rim
the pond darkens around us, and the ghosts
of you and me, barely visible off our dock,
break apart on waves beside a shifting moon.

The Lover: New Poems

For My Wife

How were we to know, leaving your two kids
behind in New Hampshire for our honeymoon
at twenty-one, that it was a trick of cheap
hotels in New York City to draw customers
like us inside by displaying a fancy lobby?
Arriving in our fourth-floor room, we found
a bed, a scarred bureau, and a bathroom door
with a cut on one side the exact shape
of the toilet bowl that was in its way
when I closed it. I opened and shut the door,
admiring the fit and despairing of it. You
discovered the initials of lovers carved
on the bureau's top in a zigzag, breaking heart.
How wrong the place was to us then,
unable to see the portents of our future
that seem so clear now in the naivete
of the arrangements we made, the hotel's
disdain for those with little money,
the carving of pain and love. Yet in that room
we pulled the covers over ourselves and lay
our love down, and in this way began our unwise
and persistent and lucky life together.

November 22, 1963

We were just starting out when it happened.
At the school where I taught the day was over.
As far as they could tell, it wouldn't be fatal.
But the principal couldn't finish the announcement.

At the school where I taught the day was over.
I had a dentist appointment right after work.
But the principal couldn't finish the announcement.
By then, we now know, the president was dead.

I had a dentist appointment right after work.
On the way, I hurried home to tell my wife.
By then, we now know, the president was dead.
I remember Jackie's pink pillbox hat in the film.

On the way, I hurried home to tell my wife.
Turn off the vacuum cleaner! I shouted at her.
I remember Jackie's pink pillbox hat in the film.
I kept thinking I was going to be late.

Turn off the vacuum cleaner! I shouted at her.
I had never made her cry like that.
I kept thinking I was going to be late.
In one frame Kennedy's head goes out of focus.

I had never made her cry like that.
The funny thing was, the dentist didn't care.
In one frame Kennedy's head goes out of focus.
We didn't realize there would soon be others.

The funny thing was, the dentist didn't care.
We were just starting out when it happened.
We didn't realize there would soon be others.
As far as they could tell, it wouldn't be fatal.

What She Means

What his daughter means
when she does it is not
good night, though it is dark
beyond the small

light where she leans
toward him
in his hospital bed,
nor could she mean

stay here with me,
for he is far away
behind his closed lids
when she touches him

where she has never
touched him, parting
and smoothing his hair,
and it is such

a private thing, this
ordinary thing she does,
her hand moving
in its memory

of how she has known him
all her life, then
drawing the johnny up
over his old collarbones

and patting it,
both hands now
going back for the pleasure
of patting it again,

though in the dark
above the small light
where I stand
close beside her

and she looks down
all alone,
what my wife means
is not what the pleased

hands mean,
her eyes wide
and swimming
and implacable.

Losing My Hair

In the old allegory of the wolves
chasing the dog sled across
the tundra in the waning

light of life, I myself
am suddenly the aging man

who must reach inside his chest
to find some failed organ
that might appease them,
though all I have now
to throw over my shoulder

is this small offering that lifts
in the wind when I turn back,
flying apart so high above them
it has nothing to do
with the gathering dark

of their bodies, and their swift
legs that barely touch the snow,
and their cold, patient eyes.

Shame

"You are beyond shame,"
my mother said after
my father left us. "What else
are you hiding?" I never told her
about the photograph

of naked women and men
in a cart beside a fence
from his book about the war,

some with hair at their crotches,
some with asses like mine,

like everyone's except,
being dead, they had nothing
to hide, and the shame
was all mine for finding them.
I went on turning its pages,

time after time, past
the portraits of generals
wearing ties like my father,
past flashes of gunfire
and rolling hills of smoke

and flame, to these
forgotten ones, lying
together in their secret, more
frightening than my mother
chasing me from couch

to chair with her switch
to make war against
her broken heart. For in this
place there was no running
or screaming. Here

nobody knew their terrible
stillness but me, the one
beyond shame, who left them
all naked, and returned
to find them, and never told.

Morning in America

What draws you to them at first is the nicknames
they have for each other and their little jokes, like
the remark the woman makes to her co-host
about his tie, then apologizes and even touches it
so she seems to more than like him, and why not,

he's handsome in a regular-guy, unthreatening
sort of way, and when they all come back
from a commercial, you almost wonder whether
the blonde who does the news might be a little
jealous, given how she keeps it up about the tie,

or maybe you think just for an instant, how is it
possible for him to watch her all dressed up in her
serious costume to read the news each morning
and not sometimes think of her "in that way,"
but when you happen to catch it the next morning,

she brings in pictures of her baby, and you say
wait a minute, she has a whole other life
off the set, this is a job and these people
are professionals, the newswoman herself,
for openers, reading right through the bad news

about all the shoppers who blew up in the open
market in Iraq and the shocking statistics about
obesity in the United States, unable no matter
how hard she tries to avoid a touch of sadness
on her face, as if what can she do besides continue

to be thin and appealing herself, which is when
you really appreciate the fat laughing guy
who does the weather because you can be serious
for just so long, and anyway there's always a silver
lining in every dark cloud, like he says, for instance

the ones hovering right here over the Midwest,
gesturing toward the cloud graphic spinning
into place, and even though everybody groans
over his corny joke including the ones behind
the camera you can't see, it sort of speaks

for the whole show, OK, the rock star can come on
to pitch her new CD but not without talking about
how she overcame depression and drug use,
and the man selling the book about his mother's
Alzheimer's has to explain how forgetting

who she was made them closer, since basically
this is all about helping you, looking in, deal with
whatever life throws at you, as the male co-host
puts it, turning between guests to his partner
while she nods thoughtfully under her hair, because

she doesn't really think of this as a job, she should be
paying the network, she says, not the other way around,
though right now they have to go to a commercial
again, not just one, of course, but ten or fifteen,
the same old thing of models pretending

they are amazed housewives or sick husbands
or doctors in lab coats saying buy this,

146

buy that, so you can't wait to get back
to some human beings who care about each other
and about us, and who are who they really are.

The Lover

Wearing a T-shirt and suspenders
in the deepening twilight as he tells me
about the house he imagines

building for the woman he imagines,
Billy Thyng is the mayor of this place
where nobody lives, town of the cowless

barn and empty chicken house
of his childhood, town of the vanishing
windows of the school bus he towed

from Wilton and couldn't start, town
of the failed truck and the trailer
he kept for his ex-wife now moved away,

as the town itself is moving away
in the dusk, school bus, chicken house,
house of his long-gone mother

and father, and even the house
he builds room by room in his mind
with his aging, gesticulating hands

that go on disappearing into the dark like
everything around him he has hoped for
and loved and never wanted to lose.

Her Secret

Why he must cover every counter top, table
and chair with his things, she no longer asks,
knowing he will only answer as if speaking
to someone in his head who's keeping track
of all the ways she misunderstands him

and wants to hear over and over that he's sick
and tired, though that's just what he is,
and how can she resent him for that? – so sick
he has pills for his bad circulation, bad heart,
and nerve disorder scattered around

the kitchen sink, so tired after staying up
all night at his computer feeding medication
to the stinging in his legs, he crashes
for one whole day into the next. "Thurman?"
she asks, coming home from work to find him

lying on their bed in his underpants, still
as the dead, his radio on to tape the talk shows
he's missing, and then the old thought
that he really is dead comes into her mind
all over again, so strong this time she can't

get rid of it, even after she sees him with her
own eyes just above the partition in the kitchen
making coffee in the way he's invented,
boiling grounds, then putting in more grounds
and a raw egg, his bald head going back

and forth under the fluorescent light like
the image of his continuous obsession,
which she can't escape and can never enter,
though now it's her own obsession
that troubles her. Stupid is her word for it,

the same word he always uses for the crazy
things she gets into her head, and it *was*
stupid, still thinking Thurman was dead
though he was right there in front of her,
and then, when she tries to make herself

stop, her heart starts pounding until
she can hardly breathe. "It is nothing more
than simple anger," the pastor tells her
after the Sunday service she attends
with the other women who live nearby,

and he recalls with disappointment
the anger he discovered in her heart
during their talk a year ago. How,
she wonders, could she have forgotten
that after she wiped away her tears

in that conversation about Thurman
leaving things he wouldn't let her touch
on every surface of the house, even
the couch and chairs, the pastor made her see
the malice she had carried so deep inside

not even she understood that all this time
she had been gradually filling the spare room
and the closed-in porch with her own
discards, broken figurines, old mops
and mop pails and Christmas decorations,

out of a secret revenge, and now,
the pastor shook his head, this thought
about her husband, whom she had pledged
to honor, lying in his underpants, dead,
the day before her fortieth anniversary.

When she returned home at last and opened
the door to find the two pairs of sneakers
next to the recliner with the ankle brace in it,
and old videos on top of the half-read
magazines and newspapers by the TV,

and the bathrobe and shirts and pants folded
over the backs of chairs, she did not feel,
as she sometimes did, that she might suffocate,
but instead, a relief that Thurman hadn't
risen yet. He wouldn't mind that she used one

of his sticky notes when he read the words
she wrote on it, *I still love you*, meaning
how sorry she was for blaming him behind
his back to the pastor, and for the secret
anger she had kept so long in her heart, yet

because, unlike most things in that house,
it was hers alone, she continued to ponder
the anger and keep it, even after Thurman took
the note from the screen of his computer
with a smile, and got his camera out

to take the anniversary photo he always took
for his emails of her holding plastic flowers,
mocking her because she never could
pose right, then sitting down among the wires
and the stacks of CDs and computer paper

to Photoshop it, going over and over her teeth
and eyes to whiten them and taking all
the wrinkles out of her face until she looked
like an old baby. "Oh, I like what you did
to it, Thurman," she said when he brought

the picture to her, sitting on her rocker in the only
clean corner of the house, and she almost meant it,
she had become so calm in her pondering, calmer
than she could ever remember as she looked
out the window and through the other window

of the closed-in porch, where a flock
of the migrating birds she loved lingered
for a time under the roof of her feeder,
and in an unaccountable moment, lifted
their wings all together and flew away.

First Snowfall

It is touching
the highest fingers
of the trees
which have longed

for it all this time,
and it is sifting down
over the store with the sign
in the window

that says Come in
we're open and the sign
on the door that says
We're closed,

and it is blowing
across the gray stacks
of lumber and the jacked-
up trailer of a semi

at Dan's Custom
Sawing, and on the Rome

Road it is coming down
on the shoulders

of telephone poles
struggling uphill carrying wire
to the double-wide
and the farmhouse

with the year-round Christmas
lights, in season once more,
and slowly, softly in the dark
it is once more

bearing down
on the old, collapsing barn
to squeeze the row
of windows

shut, nobody up
to see it fill the driveways
and walkways except
a snowplow

holding a small light
ahead of itself opening the street
that vanishes in the long
drift and dream

of it, coming down
over the whole town
where everyone
under every

last, lost
roof is now far away
and all gone
and good night.

Love Story

What was opening the door
those years ago to let our four kids
one by one followed by the dog
into the back seat of the old compact car
we'd parked in the driveway
next to the down-hill road because
the battery went dead the day before –
what, but a prayer?

What were our arguments
as we tried to time my pushing
the family down the road and your
taking your foot off the clutch
to start the car, though instead bringing it
to a dead stop over and over –
what, but an agreement to go on
despite our limitations?

What was the moment
in the midst of our despair
when the engine suddenly caught
and you roared away and came back
for me, and I got in by the soda can

on the floor and the dog now sitting
between us on the emergency brake,
the whole family smiling

as the trees broke apart faster and faster
above our heads – what, but a blessing?

ACKNOWLEDGMENTS

Thanks to the University of Missouri Press for permission to reprint poems from *The Faces of Americans in 1853*, copyright © 1983 by Wesley McNair.

Thanks to David R. Godine, Publisher, Inc., for twenty-five years of support, and for permission to reprint poems from the following collections: *The Town of No*, copyright © 1989 by Wesley McNair; *My Brother Running*, copyright © 1993 by Wesley McNair; *Talking in the Dark*, copyright © 1998 by Wesley McNair; *Fire*, copyright © 2002 by Wesley McNair; *The Ghosts of You and Me*, copyright © 2006 by Wesley McNair.

My gratitude also to the following magazines, where new poems originally appeared: *Agni* online: "First Snowfall" ; *Five Points*: "For My Wife," "November 22, 1963"; *Green Mountains Review*: "The Lover"; *Margie*: "Her Secret," "Love Story," "Morning in America," "What She Means"; *Slate*: "Losing My Hair"; *Sewanee Review*: "Shame."

Final thanks to United States Artists for a USA fellowship that helped me complete this book, to Robert Kimber and David Scribner for help with manuscript preparation, and to the following readers who assisted with selections: Donald Hall, Peter Harris, Mike Pride, Philip Schultz and Thomas Smith.

ABOUT THE AUTHOR

WESLEY MCNAIR's volumes of poetry include seven collections and two limited editions. He has also published books of prose and anthologies of Maine writing. A recipient of Fulbright and Guggenheim fellowships, he has received two NEA grants and has twice been awarded Rockefeller fellowships for creative work at the Bellagio Center in Italy. His honors in poetry include the Theodore Roethke Prize, the Eunice Tietjens Prize, the Jane Kenyon Award and the Sarah Josepha Hale Medal. In 2006 he was awarded a United States Artists fellowship for poetry. He lives with his wife, Diane, in Mercer, Maine.

A NOTE ON THE TYPE

*Lovers of the Lost has been set in Adobe Systems'
Warnock Pro, an OpenType font first designed in 1997 by
Robert Slimbach. Named for John Warnock, one of Adobe's
founders, the roman was originally intended for its name-
sake's personal use, but was later developed into a compre-
hensive family of types. Although the type is based firmly in
Slimbach's calligraphic work, the completed family makes
abundant use of the refinements attainable via digitization.
With its range of weights and optical sizes, Warnock Pro is
elegant in display settings, warm and readable at text sizes
– a classical design with contemporary adaptability.*

DESIGN & COMPOSITION BY CARL W. SCARBROUGH